Let Me Help You

Let Me Help You

Poetic Bible Truths About Living Life

✺

ERIC ZACK

RESOURCE *Publications* · Eugene, Oregon

LET ME HELP YOU
Poetic Bible Truths About Living Life

Resource Publications
An Imprint of Wipf and Stock Publishers
199 W. 8th Ave., Suite 3
Eugene, OR 97401

www.wipfandstock.com

PAPERBACK ISBN: 979-8-3852-3352-6
HARDCOVER ISBN: 979-8-3852-3353-3
EBOOK ISBN: 979-8-3852-3354-0

VERSION NUMBER 12/10/24

Contents

Choice

Prayer

The Gift of Life

Blessings

Preface

Welcome to my private collection of Christian poetry spanning five total volumes and 173 original, unique poems that I have written over the past thirty years of my life. Each volume deals with key aspects of Christianity and Holy Bible truths that have been revealed to me during my personal struggles. I have organized each one of these into an easy-to-read-and-follow format. Certain lines and stanzas in each of these poems will also have specific Bible verses referenced if you prefer to investigate further, meditate, or dive deeper into the Word.

Volume 1 focuses on God, the Bible, and surrendering. Volume 2 describes Jesus Christ and the need to be born again. Volume 3 highlights important Christian tenants that support living life to its fullest, such as grace, faith, choice, prayer, life, and blessings. Volume 4 depicts evil such as rebellion, pride, Satan, disease, death, and hell. And finally, volume 5 completes my collection with living for the future by applying Christian beliefs and putting this lifestyle into practice in serving others. It covers topics such as the Church, correction, redemption, finding purpose, the rapture, heaven, and the end of times.

I have generally written these poems whenever I had ideas or inspirations come to me and when I had the time to process them, sit down, and compose them (preferably in an uninterrupted manner). Although their actual chronological order has been lost, I feel that there is great benefit in how these poems have been organized for your understanding and reading pleasure. My brain seems to work in this manner by compartmentalizing related topics together. My intention was to document many of my own personal experiences along with my spiritual growth journey, not that I am anyone special in that respect. I'm just an ordinary person whose life experiences have opened my eyes to Jesus at an early point in my young adult life due to certain circumstances. I am so grateful for what has happened in my life and that I was chosen worthy by Jesus to suffer through extreme emotional pain. This has directly led me towards Him. My mom's death was absolutely the worst thing that has ever happened to me; yet in retrospect, it was absolutely the best thing that has ever happened to me. This stark dichotomy remains quite perplexing to me. But I have always wanted to learn what the truth is.

My typical poetry style is to tell an impactful story with powerful emotional details that describe a specific defined topic; and most of them possess some rhythm and rhyming pattern based on the melodies of contemporary music. My hope is that they inspire and speak to you and specifically the younger generation— who might appreciate this form of expression. Most of my poems have been adapted as such, changing the lyrics of these songs to reveal important Bible truths. These melodies are also referenced next to my poem titles. But all of these poems are stand-alone, in that without the melody, they should still make perfect sense. Most of my poems are nonfictional (based on real-life experiences as either being autobiographical or biographical in context); while some are completely fictional (made-up to highlight a particular truth). None of these types really matter in order to highlight the main theme of each poem, nor have these been revealed. One secret I have learned over the years about growing closer to Christ is found in Rom 10:17: "So then faith *comes* by hearing, and hearing by the word of God" (NKJV, italics original). This can be accomplished in many ways and whichever ways you choose; these are pleasing to Him.

I considered my life pretty normal growing up until my mom's death. Then seemingly overnight, my world fell apart, and I felt lost and confused. I didn't know what was happening to me. I asked typical questions like, Why me? and, Why now?, but nothing was revealed to me. Shortly thereafter, my stepfather struggled with alcoholism as a way to self-medicate and numb the emotional pain that he was feeling. And the four of us kids were left to fend for ourselves for our own survival.

I returned to college but barely passed the remaining semesters of my first degree. Nothing as serious as this has ever occurred to me before or ever since thankfully. I was surviving one day at a time and learning valuable lessons as I went through the grieving process internally and privately. It was a slow process for me, as I was still learning who I was, developing into who I wanted to become, all while being a young teenager at heart. All of a sudden, I had to grow up and do so really fast . . . and on my own. Poetry was the only thing that worked for me. Back then, no one had cell phones, and the internet was just created a few years prior to this. Moreover, all of my childhood friends were back in my hometown or away at another college. None of my new college acquaintances could understand what I was going through. Indeed, I felt all alone. Poetry was my only outlet. Putting my emotions down on paper seemed to give these abstract things actual weight, relevance, and true acknowledgment. It also allowed me to literally (physically) and figuratively (emotionally) store my emotions away—as if to feel them, deal with them, learn from them, and then move on from them.

My original intention was simply to try to heal myself—deep down knowing that if I continued to bottle up these emotions over time, I would eventually explode just like a boiling pot of water in a kettle on the stovetop. Introverts need time, privacy, and quiet to process difficult experiences. I did not trust anyone enough to share these vulnerabilities with—for fear of judgment, criticism, or simply being dismissed. I never thought my poems would ultimately be worthy of sharing with others to help them in some way. In the midst of tragedy, you can only think of yourself. However, once you pass through that tragedy, you eventually regain a sense of others in the world and can see life and future possibilities and new opportunities more clearly. My hope and prayers are that my poems can help some of you in whatever you are facing today, whether it be serious or trivial, permanent or temporary, or spiritual, psychosocial, and/or physical. I now realize that Jesus was the only one who could heal me and not as a result of my own efforts. My efforts only proved to be futile attempts to try to do what only God can do. I have learned this valuable lesson to let go of certain things that I cannot control.

I have continued writing poetry on a regular basis about life's many experiences, topics, and questions. It has become and remains to be a strong coping mechanism for me when dealing with "life." I have continued to develop and refine my writing abilities and have strengthened my art by adding, practicing, and improving on many tools in my toolbox, so to speak. Sharing these Christian poems has become my priority given today's troubling times with so many broken and lost people. Jesus is the answer to all of your questions!

Introduction

Welcome to the third volume of my Christian poetry collection. It is entitled *Let Me Help You: Poetic Bible Truths About Living Life*. This collection focuses on living today in the present moment—specifically about grace, faith, choice, prayer, life, and blessings.

The first section in this book begins with grace. Grace is undeserved, unmerited favor. As human beings, we deserve nothing but death. But instead, God offers us His rich mercy by not giving us what we rightly deserve, but rather He offers us His inexhaustible supply and saving grace, rewarding His obedient children in this lifetime and beyond (Col 3:23-24; Jas 1:12; Matt 5:12; 1 Cor 3:10-17).

The second section describes faith. Faith is the belief and/or trust in God based on evidence but without total proof. Hebrews 11:1 describes faith as the assurance (title deed, confirmation) of things hoped for (divinely guaranteed) and the evidence of things not seen.

The third section depicts choice. We are all given free will and free choice to do and think as we please, given certain common-sense confines such as not impinging on someone else's rights or their free will. But just as a parent is drawn to their child who chooses to spend time with them, to follow their advice or example, and to make them proud, so too does God lean towards those who make Him to be a priority in their lives. Our choices have consequences.

The fourth section deals with prayer. Prayer is the open admission that without Christ Jesus we can do nothing on our own. Prayer is an expression of faith in God's power, fueled by a desire for more of Him. Praying your way through the day is a common practice of many Christians. Although we cannot impact or steer everything correctly, God can. Prayer is asking Him for help in doing what we cannot do ourselves, understanding our limits while at the same time understanding His power. "With God all things are possible" (Matt 19:26 NIV).

The fifth section highlights life. Life is a precious gift from God. "And the Lord God formed man of the dust of the ground and breathed into his nostrils the breath of life; and man became a living soul" (Gen 2:7 KJV). Moreover, God promises "before I formed you in the womb I knew you" (Jer 1:5 NIV). In Eccl 12:7, it is stated that "the dust returns to the ground it came from, and the spirit returns to God who gave it" (NIV). We only have one life to live. How will you live your life? Who will you live your life for? What is the meaning of life? Do you cherish the gift of life?

The final section focuses on blessings. We are blessed with so many things if we really sit and meditate on all that we truly have. Many of us look to our neighbors, "the Joneses," so to speak, as a comparison of what we should or could have, what we should or could want, what we might not or don't have. In America, it's easy to take your eyes off the ball and view physical possessions and other temporal or worldly things as determining happiness, success, or fulfillment. But God desires that we shift our focus to the eternal or spiritual realm instead. "So, we fix our eyes not on what is seen, but on what is unseen, since what is seen is temporary, but what is unseen is eternal" (2 Cor 4:18 NIV). Friendships, respect, kindness, love, health, and identifying our spiritual gifts and employing them to benefit others are key aspects of building up your eternal account. "To one there is given through the Spirit a message of wisdom, to another a message of knowledge by means of the same Spirit, to another faith by the same Spirit, to another gifts of healing by that one Spirit, to another miraculous powers, to another prophecy, to another distinguishing between spirits, to another speaking in different kinds of tongues, and to still another the interpretation of tongues" (1 Cor 12:8–10 NIV). Temporal things will eventually all cease to exist. What is eternal will be tested with fire and remain.

Thank you and may God bless you. Please enjoy!

GRACE

Sanctification

(Adapted from the melody of "Doves" by Future Islands)

I don't know what's wrong
hard to smile, I don't belong
can't breathe, disturbed
color blind in a color world
what was hoped versus what has become
time passes until we succumb
keep going forward, forget the past
hold onto hope in contrast
tomorrow always comes
then the sun will shine once more
can't recreate happiness
so, work harder; busyness
memories gone, now forgotten
no desire, uncommon
routines always the same
repeat, so mundane
think I've developed an aversion
to life and others, need a diversion
time's running out, can this be reversed?
not sure, maybe cursed
miss joy, miss fun
miss laughter, miss everyone
childhood dreams now lost
what was an open book, now crushed
children all grown up
look in the mirror, interrupt
find myself, misjudge
What's different? Not much
What's next? Who knows?
uphill or plateau
surrender or continue to fight
Disgraced? Look up   Ps 14:2
seek another whom to trust   Ps 118:8–14

there's only one who instructs
who has all the answers, deep thoughts   1 Chr 29:11–13
countless prayers, see the cross   Gal 2:20
I need your help, please fix me
one of these days remedy
tunnel vision, see distant light
out of darkness into the bright   1 John 1:5
God's always working each new day
be patient, He'll provide the way   John 14:6
curved path, destination
round the corner—sanctification   2 Tim 2:21

Not Worthy

(Adapted from the melody of "Unsteady" by X Ambassadors)

Save, save me, save me from myself	
'Cause I'm just not worthy, I'm not worthy	Matt 8:8
Save, save me, save me from myself	
'Cause I'm just not worthy, I'm not worthy	

My God, help me	
Approach, no fear	Isa 41:10
You sit there on Your throne	Ps 11:4
Why You care for me—unknown	
'Cause Your love for me overflows	1 John 4:16
'Cause You love me, now I know	

Raise, raise me, raise me up to You	1 John 4:9–10
'Cause I'm just not worthy, I'm not worthy	
Raise, raise me, raise me up to You	
'Cause I'm just not worthy. I'm not worthy	

Father, I've learned	
To trust You and return	Prov 3:5–6
LORD, I know You're forgiving	2 Cor 5:19
See past me, Your Son's fulfilling	Col 3:3

Because you love me, mercy flows	Eph 2:4–5
'Cause You love me, grace bestowed	John 1:17

Hold, hold on, hold onto me
'Cause I'm just not worthy, I'm not worthy
Hold, hold on, hold onto me
'Cause I'm just not worthy, I'm not worthy

Free, free me, free me from my sins
'Cause I'm just not worthy, I'm not worthy

Living Under Grace Compared to The Law

God is triune, so let's discuss this mysterious crew   Gen 1:26

God is perfect and holy, thus your nearness is denied   1 Sam 2:2
His commandments exist and you must comply   Exod 20
You're guilty if any of these you don't apply   Jas 2:10
You're doomed to hell this implies   Rom 6:23

You have to find a way to undo (undo)   John 14:6
You need a substitute, start anew (anew)   1 Pet 3:18
His demands are impossible, but He supplies the truth for you to
     pursue (pursue)

God gave us His Son just to provide (provide)   Heb 10:9–10
To be close to you and to be your guide (guide)
The impossible becomes possible in lieu (in lieu, in lieu, in lieu)
     Matt 19:26

God said that I am the Lord, and you shall have no other Gods
     apart   Exod 20:3
But Jesus implored us to love God with all your heart   Deut 6:5
God declared that you shall not steal, and the world teaches us to
     be thrift   Exod 20:15
But Jesus taught us to love and give and forgive lest you not be
     forgiven   John 13:34

God bought you with a price, placed all your sins on
     Jesus Christ   1 Cor 6:12–20
He was punished for you, He was crucified   Matt 27:34–35
Creating that divine transaction whereby
You became righteous overnight   2 Cor 5:21

You have to find a way to undo (undo)
You need a substitute, start anew (anew)
His demands are impossible, but He supplies the truth for you to
    pursue (pursue)

God gave us His Son just to provide (provide)
To be close to you and to be your guide (guide)
The impossible becomes possible in lieu (in lieu, in lieu, in lieu)

Yes, God's in you   1 John 4:12
Yes, the Holy Spirit's in you   1 Cor 6:19

God ordained to keep the Lord's Day, while Jesus said the Sabbath
    was for man   Mark 2:27
God said not to take My name in vain, yet your sins were
    cleansed by Jesus's name   1 John 1:7–9
God said not to bear false witness or covet your neighbor's wife
    or goods
But Jesus said not to worry about your life,   Matt 6:25–34
What you'll eat, or the clothes you'll buy
You have to find a way to undo (undo)
You need a substitute, start anew (anew)
His demands are impossible, but He supplies the truth for you to
    pursue (pursue)

God gave us His Son just to provide (provide)
To be close to you and to be your guide (guide)
The impossible becomes possible in lieu (in lieu, in lieu, in lieu)

God said to honor your parents, respect both your mom and dad
And by doing so, Jesus as a child grew in favor with God
They were anxiously searching for Him, didn't know where he
    was or understand
But He was obedient to them   Luke 2:42–51
And grew in stature and wisdom

You have to find a way to undo (undo)
You need a substitute, start anew (anew)
His demands are impossible, but He supplies the truth for you to
pursue (pursue)

God gave us His Son just to provide (provide)
To be close to you and to be your guide (guide)
The impossible becomes possible in lieu (in lieu, in lieu, in lieu)

Yes, God's in you
Yes, the Holy Spirit's in you

God declared that you shall not kill
But Jesus said love your neighbor as though   Matt 22:39
God said do not commit adultery, but then alternatively Jesus
spoke
As Christ loved the Church, husbands please love your wives Eph
5:25–33
And wives submit to your husbands hereby
Just like the Church submits to Christ   Eph 5:22–24

You have to find a way to undo (undo)
You need a substitute, start anew (anew)
His demands are impossible, but He supplies the truth for you to
pursue (pursue)

God gave us His Son just to provide (provide)
To be close to you and to be your guide (guide)
The impossible becomes possible in lieu (in lieu, in lieu, in lieu)

Not Under Law

(Adapted from the melody of "As It Was" by Harry Styles)

I'm under attack
Eventually I will bounce back
The media's screaming compliance, they demand
Why do great things get hijacked?

No room to stray
Or you will be faced with dismay
Cancelled or even erased
Next to become their prey, oh-oh-oh   1 Pet 5:8

It's confirmed, sin withdrawn
You know we're really not under law   Rom 6:14
It's confirmed, sin withdrawn
You know we're really not under law
Under law, under law
You know we're really not . . .

A house built on stone   Luke 6:48
The LORD sitting on His throne   Ps 11:4
What exactly have you asked for?
What kinds of seeds have you sown?   Matt 13:18–23

Do you want to go to hell?
Truth be told and lies dispelled
Think you can save yourself?   Ps 146:3
The Holy Spirit must indwell, oh-oh-oh   Rom 8:9

It's confirmed, sin withdrawn
You know we're really not under law
It's confirmed, sin withdrawn
You know we're really not under law
Under law, under law
You know we're really not . . .

Punished, his skin shed; He truly paid all your debt   Isa 53:5
He did all of this for you just because
And now all you have to do is simply believe   Rom 10:9
Receive His grace and redemption through His blood   Eph 1:7

Under law, you know we're really not under law
Under law, under law

Graduated

(Adapted from the melody of "Me Myself & I" by 5 Seconds of Summer)

I'm sick; I've been diagnosed with leukemia
Infection and bleeding
Treated with chemicals to the point of physical and emotional
  depletion

New mom, I was a new mom and felt distraught
But I was surrounded with amazing support
So scared; news of my disease relapse left me defeated

"Six months to live" overwhelmed
It's like they ignited dynamite
I'm not ready for my farewell

"A bone marrow transplant or you will die"
"A bone marrow transplant or you will die"
"A bone marrow transplant or you will die"

No choice, I just had to confront this
The treatment went well and succeeded
The medical report was clean when I finally reached completion

Grateful that I survived this assault   Eph 6:12
Thankful for the things that this has taught
I was spared. Is this really true or have I been dreaming?

I'm mad that Satan compelled   Gen 50:20
For life's not always black and white
All of his lies were dispelled   John 8:44

God answered my precious prayers, but "Why?"   Ps 34:17–18
God answered my precious prayers, but "Why?"
God answered my precious prayers, but "Why?"

This test's over; I ponder, what an honor
The little things superseded

It's funny how this propelled
Given all that we have sacrificed
The most important things were upheld
Everyone keeps saying that I was so brave

I don't worry about my blood cells
My daughter's now eighteen; I'm tongue-tied
Under Christ's wings we have dwelled   Ps 57:1

And I watched her graduate tonight!
And I watched her graduate tonight!
And I watched her graduate tonight!

FAITH

Spiritual Sight

(Adapted from the melody of "One" by Metallica)

I woke up again with clouded vision
I can only make out bright light beams
I can't do much, walking is extreme
The eye pain constantly bothers me

My reflection in the mirror I can't see
The pressure builds, I'm down on one knee
Even my wife's face escapes me
There must be a reason that You'd allow   Rom 8:28

I pray for You to give me the strength   Ps 18
Oh, please God: Mercy?

Too many eye drops, one more appeal
My daily life feels so surreal
Waiting for surgery, possibly to heal
I sometimes think that I only exist

I ask what's the purpose, "why me?" audibly
Not sure how much longer honestly
Could there be anything good possibly?
Then something appears to the contrary:

Lose my sight, but gain eternal life   John 10:27–28
Oh, please God: Save me!

With my eyes shut, spiritual sight's been thrust
Oh, God has blessed me!
Lose my sight, but gain eternal life
Oh, thank God: He saved me!

Through this, God chose me	John 15:16
He heard my pleas, my faith's stronger,	Ps 34:17–18
Jesus Christ gave; With His cross, I died	Rom 6:3–4
I surrender myself	Matt 16:24–26
Totally, my soul's immortal	1 Cor 15:51–55

I'm aligned, I stand upright	
I can now preach, testimony sharing	Acts 1:8
Satan's disarmed, I no longer beg	Jas 4:7
God's in control	Eph 1:11
I may be blind, but I can see	
Oh, praise God: He saved me! God Himself has saved me!	

You Must Believe

(Adapted from the melody of "A Song for Our Grandfathers" by Future Islands)

Every single day, people are dying
Surrounded by loved ones who are crying
Their souls leave quietly
This moment's so defining
And then it's done
So, what happens now?

Is death the end, or is it just the beginning of something else?
I ponder this
Is it dark? A deep abyss?
Or greeted by a bright light with Jesus who's welcoming
I can't dismiss   John 14:2–6

It all depends on if you believe   Acts 16:31
He said: "Please come to me.   Matt 11:28
Don't you want to be free?   Rom 6:18
Just be brave.
You must believe   Acts 16:31
or there's no guarantee."

I sit there with wet tissues in my hands
Staring down at the tile floor; the shadows dance
There used to be laughter
It's hard to understand
But death is the price of our sin's unholy demand

The sting has been taken away   1 Cor 15:55–58
As Jesus has conquered death   Matt 28
This He did
Resurrected after his last breath
He rose as He said, a doorway that we pass through   Acts 2:24
To spend eternity with God and avoid His wrath   John 14:19

It all depends on if you believe
And He said: "Please come to me.
Don't you want to be free?
Just be brave.
You must believe
or there's no guarantee."

There's nothing to fear   Isa 41:10
When Jesus is near   Jas 4:8
There's nothing to fear
When Jesus is near

We'll all face death soon   Heb 9:27
With other eyes watching you
Will you feel safe?
Will you feel safe?

I Try To Relax While I Run

Holding my head up, slow breaths with each step
Music in my ears, my mind wanders in depth
There's no tension in my face, thumbs cradled in my hands
Such a gentle grip, the landscape expands

I discovered this secret, taught by my coach
Revealed its meaning, bigger in life than in sports

No stress in my back, my left foot and then my right
Elbows driven back and down, weightless and light
Each stride is the same, with a slight lean forward
Always focused on proper form, never landing awkward

Faith is my currency with a future view   Gal 2:20
I see things clearly occur before they come true

I think of the cross, I pray often while I run
I live in the moment; in Him, all things are done   Phil 4:13
I ask if He is able, He answers me: "Yes"
"Father, are You willing?" Again, He answers me: "Yes" Matt 8:1–3

Because I trust You; Yes, I trust You   John 14:1
Oh, how I trust You

Although I am sweating; in Him, my soul finds restMatt 11:28–30
His grace greatly abounds, I know that I am blessed   Rom 5:20
He protects my whole body; He supplies me with favor   Phil 4:19
Indeed, He's my rock, my fortress, and my Savior   Luke 19:10

I envision His sacrifice, His desire to take my place   1 Cor 15:3–8
The pain and suffering He chose, and now my sins are erased
                                                          Heb 8:12

I follow His lead, a true partner with Christ   1 Pet 4:13
Surrendering to His will, in awe of His might   Prov 3:5–6
It's sort of like when I try to relax when I run
I softly share my requests, He won't be outdone

Because I trust You; Yes, I trust You
Oh, how I trust You

I have given Him pre-eminence in my life   Mark 12:30
Every day starts the same, I seek His advice   Phil 4:6
I let Him work through me, regardless of the task   Gal 2:20
Let all the power, praise, and glory point to Jesus Christ   Rev 7:12

I Am in Christ Jesus, Risen

(Adapted from the melody of "Nothing Really Matters" by Madonna)

God has so many names
Described and hidden within the Bible
Some are completely distant
Others are much more intimate

We must all decide
Which name we will use
In context to our relationship
When referring to Him

El Olam, El Shaddai,	Gen 21:33; Gen 17:1
Elohim, Adonai,	Ps 82; Judges 6:15
El Elyon, Jehovah	Gen 14:18–24; Ps 83:18
Yud Hei Vav Hei, Yahweh;	Exod 3; Gen 1:1–2
but Abba is His secret name	Gal 4:6

We are all His creation	Gen 1:27
He wants us to love Him deeply	
He surrenders us our free will	1 John 1:8–10
To make up our own minds	

He loves us so
To do this for us
He accepts our decisions
But at our peril

El Olam, El Shaddai, Elohim, Adonai, El Elyon, Jehovah
Yud Hei Vav Hei, Yahweh; but Abba is His secret name

Depending on where you place Him
Or how much exposed
Depending on what you truly believe
Or how close
You can select His namesake
And He will respect your claim

El Olam, El Shaddai, Elohim, Adonai, El Elyon, Jehovah
Yud Hei Vav Hei, Yahweh; but Abba is His secret name

From My Pillow

(Adapted from the melody of "Anti-Hero" by Taylor Swift)

When I wake up, I remember my dreams and then try to analyze
   them
But soon I reset; my day resumes
Most people will live out their lives with minimal retrieval
Forget their dreams until death looms

Important things often come in many disguises
It could be the Messiah to surprise you   Job 33:14–18
So don't just simply deny this during the nighttime

And while I'm sleeping, I'm breathing
I wander the universe seeking meaning
My understanding's slowly increasing during the nighttime

Lift me high, please won't You set me free   Gal 5:1
Before I die, wake me up spiritually   Luke 22:46
Too many people are too attached to their material possessions
This must be so daunting; all of this is revealed from my pillow

I describe it like the walking dead aimlessly roaming daily
Boldly expressing their free will
No one's listening, even though I'm screaming quite loudly
There's a fresh start if you want to be filled

Young people cling to their idealism calling everything racism
They're unaware of their extremism during the daytime

And while I'm sleeping, I'm breathing
I wander the universe seeking meaning
My understanding's slowly increasing during the nighttime

Lift me high, please won't You set me free
Before I die, wake me up spiritually

Too many people are too attached to their material possessions
This must be so daunting; all of this is revealed from my pillow

Reality's not as important as their phone is, though it's not funny
They're always looking for a thrill
They may never realize the true meaning of this life is others
Mark 12:30–31
They think the answer's in a pill

Lift me high, please won't You set me free
Lift me high, please won't You set me free
Before I die, wake me up spiritually
Wake me up spiritually

Lift me high, please won't You set me free
Before I die, wake me up spiritually
Too many people are too attached to their material possessions
This must be so daunting; all of this is revealed from my pillow

The Window

God exists
Just like the sun exists
If you are indoors or in a dark room, you can deny that the sun
    exists
It's true that you can't see its brightness or feel its warmth
But the sun still exists despite your claims
You just refuse to acknowledge the truth
To err is human
We are indeed ignorant beings—to be lacking in knowledge or
    awareness
"Your truth" is not necessarily THY truth
It's all based on perspective
And Man's perspective is little, confined, shunted, and brief
Faith on the other hand is the complete trust or confidence in
    someone or something
Faith is like a window   1 Cor 13:12
The window lets the sunlight in
The window lets the warmth circulate
The bigger your faith, the bigger your window
Big windows let in a lot of light and warmth
And thus, the more God can do in your life   Jer 29:11
"Now faith is the assurance of things hoped for, the conviction of
    things not seen"   Heb 11:1[1]
Thomas was an unbelieving disciple of Jesus   John 20:24–29
He said, "Unless I see the nail marks in his hands and put my
    finger where the nails were, and put my hand into his side, I
    will not believe."
But Jesus appeared to him and said "Put your finger here; see
    my hands. Reach out your hand and put it into my side. Stop
    doubting and believe."

1. ESV.

Moreover, Jesus concluded, "Because you have seen me, you have believed; blessed are those who have not seen and yet have believed."   John 20:25–26, 29[2]

"For we walk by faith, not by sight"   2 Cor 5:7[3]

When Jesus had entered Capernaum, a centurion came to him, asking for help. "Lord," he said, "my servant lies at home paralyzed, suffering terribly."

"Jesus said to him, 'Shall I come and heal him?'"

"The centurion replied, 'Lord, I do not deserve to have you come under my roof. But just say the word, and my servant will be healed.'"

"Then Jesus said to the centurion, 'Go! Let it be done just as you believed it would.' And his servant was healed at that moment." Matt 8:7–8, 13[4]

"So faith comes from hearing, and hearing through the word of Christ"   Rom 10:17[5]

Jesus said, "Unless you believe that I am who I claim to be, you will die in your sins."   John 8:24[6]

"If you declare with your mouth, 'Jesus is Lord,' and believe in your heart that God raised him from the dead, then you will be saved."   Rom 10:9[7]

"And without faith it is impossible to please God, because anyone who comes to him must believe that he exists and that he rewards those who earnestly seek him."   Heb 11:6[8]

"Yet we know that a person is not justified by works of the law but through faith in Jesus Christ, so we also have believed in Christ Jesus, in order to be justified by faith in Christ and not

2. NIV.
3. KJV.
4. NIV.
5. ESV.
6. NLT.
7. ICB.
8. NIV.

by works of the law, because by works of the law no one will be justified." Gal 2:16[9]

"And whatever you ask in prayer, you will receive, if you have faith" Matt 21:22[10]

"Because nothing shall be impossible with God" Luke 1:37[11]

"The righteous will live by faith." Rom 1:17[12]

"For by grace, you have been saved through faith. And this is not your own doing; it is the gift of God, not a result of works, so that no one may boast." Eph 2:8–9[13]

"Whoever believes in me, as Scripture has said, rivers of living water will flow from within them." John 7:38[14]

Be on guard; stand firm in the faith; be courageous; be strong. 1 Cor 16:13[15]

"In the same way, let your light shine before others, so that they may see your good works and give glory to your Father in heaven." Matt 5:16[16]

How big is your window?

9. ESV.
10. ESV.
11. YLT.
12. NIV.
13. ESV.
14. NIV.
15. NIV.
16. CSB.

Don't Bother with the Whys

(Adapted from the melody of "Goodbyes" by Post Malone, feat. Young Thug)

When I've suffered and sustained, it's too easy to blame
I feel tired and drained, and my words are profane
I just want things explained; I'm standing on a ledge

I've had enough outright, and God feels like He's out of touch
Am I being punished or judged? I just want to throw it all away

Stay in the now instead
Don't dwell on the past, but focus on what's ahead
There's no way to see God's view   Isa 55:8–9
I need to continue and move through
Don't bother with the Whys   Phil 4:6–7

Psychological pain, I just want to complain
I don't want to remain and increase my disdain
I'm not entertained; I'm considering revenge

But looking back with hindsight
I was so limited and myopic
I wished God were just a little bit more responsive
Each day was and a struggle and exhaustive
Yet, I have honor

Stay in the now instead
Don't dwell on the past, but focus on what's ahead
There's no way to see God's view
I need to continue and move through; don't bother with the
    Whys

There're more chapters to write
I have a little more fight
God promised me abundant life   John 10:10

28

It would be nice for me to invite
Him to guide my steps hereafter despite   Ps 37:23–24
God promised me that things would turn out alright   Ps 55:22

You prefer "Father," you're my main patriarch   Gal 4:6
You're the creator, the top of the hierarch   Col 1:16–17
You don't want me deprived to continue to wander   Deut 8:3
Instead, you want me alive and healthy to prosper   Gen 39:3

An answer may never come in this lifetime
God is sovereign; He has His own paradigm   Eph 1:11

An answer may never come in this lifetime
Just surrender, no more fighting   Jas 4:7
There's still plenty of time to reunite

Stay in the now instead
Don't dwell on the past, but focus on what's ahead
There's no way to see God's view
I need to continue and move through
Don't bother with the Whys

Child-like Faith

(Adapted from the melody of "Loving You" by Cannons)

Some might say that this is dumb:	
Revert back to a child, and how come?	Matt 18:3
Are you flesh or spirit akin?	Job 10:4
What exactly do you believe in?	John 14:11

Which desires do you pursue?	
Do you know, do you have a clue?	
You have no idea you're blind	John 9:41
You can open your eyes and find	Eph 1:18

To humbly trust that this world is bust, then enter heaven as His	
heir	Rom 8:17

An expected return, God's longing	Eccl 12:8
He simply asks that you choose	Deut 30:19
What compares? Whom do you belong to?	Rom 12:5
There's no excuse; do you seek truth?	John 7:18
What do you have to lose?	Luke 9:25

Curiosity and love	1 John 4:16
Like the innocent Son	Luke 23:14
Resurrection through baptism:	Acts 1:22
This is what Christ has done	John 11:26

There's so much at stake	
He offers His free grace	John 1:17
There's only one escape by design	1 Cor 10:13

An expected return, God's longing
He simply asks that you choose
What compares? Whom do you belong to?
There's no excuse; do you seek truth?
What do you have to lose?

To humbly trust that this world is bust, then enter heaven as His
    heir

An expected return, God's longing
He simply asks that you choose
What compares? Whom do you belong to?
There is no excuse; do you seek truth?
What do you have to lose?

By The Cross

(Adapted from the melody of "Lost" by Maroon 5)

There's a disconnection because of our rejection of Law	Isa 59:2
Reversing and preserving a different, He foresaw	John 14:6

He provided a way of escape, a way of escape	1 Cor 10:13
And all you have to do is proclaim Jesus' name	Rom 10:13-15

By the cross, by the cross, by the cross, He determined that I'm	Luke 14:27
heaven bound, heaven bound, heaven bound	1 John 3:2
All of my sins He erased through faith, I'm surrounded by His love	Ps 103:12
At a cost, by the cross; I've been crowned	2 Tim 2:12

By the cross, by the cross, by the cross, He determined that I'm
heaven bound, heaven bound, heaven bound
All of my sins He erased through faith, I'm surrounded by His
love
At a cost, by the cross; I've been crowned

Grateful to be chosen, I used to be in dire straits	Col 3:12
I was once broken, I was once a real disgrace	Zeph 3:17
He took my place, He took my place	
	2 Cor 5:21
And so, Jesus was betrayed, Jesus was betrayed	Matt 26:15
Thus, I'm no longer ashamed	Rom 1:16
We're His bridesmaid	Isa 54:5

By the cross, by the cross, by the cross, He determined that I'm
heaven bound, heaven bound, heaven bound
All of my sins He erased through faith, I'm surrounded by His
love

At a cost, by the cross; I've been crowned

By the cross, by the cross, by the cross, He determined that I'm
heaven bound, heaven bound, heaven bound
All of my sins He erased through faith, I'm surrounded by His
love
At a cost, by the cross; I've been crowned

There's no need to be afraid, no need to be afraid Josh 1:9; Ps 23:4
We'll return to Him again, then together we'll reign   Rev 20:4

By the cross, by the cross, by the cross, He determined that I'm
heaven bound, heaven bound, heaven bound
All of my sins He erased through faith, I'm surrounded by His
love
At a cost, by the cross; I've been crowned

By the cross, by the cross, by the cross, He determined that I'm
heaven bound, heaven bound, heaven bound
All of my sins He erased through faith, I'm surrounded by His
love
At a cost, by the cross; I've been crowned

CHOICE

You Decide

(Adapted from the melody of "Decide" by Pet Shop Boys)

criticized?
cast aside?
petrified?
compromised?
Recognize, realize, minimize, and simplify
open your eyes, utilize, you're qualified, now modify
be crucified
then purified
amplified
dignified
justified
bona-fide
magnified
and fortified
occupied
verified
unified
and satisfied
now testify
edify
glorify
and sanctify

Riding The Escalator Down

We are all riding the escalator down
It is several stories long with several intersecting areas
As soon as we are born, we actually begin to die   Eccl 3:2
We are also born with original sin—   Rom 5:12
A consequence from Adam and Eve's disobedience to God while
    in Eden
It's the price we must pay because God is just and therefore, He
    must punish sin   Rom 6:23
And we sin because we are sinners
It's in our blood   Rom 5:12
Our sin prevents us from being in God's presence because He is
    Holy
And our sentence is death
We are on our way down to Hell
Hell is our "just" destination
It is what we deserve
And although no one has ever been there and returned to
    describe it
Jesus spoke about Hell more than anyone else in the Bible
And Jesus cannot lie
This is what He said: Hell is a real place—   Mark 9:48
                    Hell is a place of judgment—   Matt 25:41; 2
                                      Thess 1:9
                    Hell is forever—   Mark 9:43
                    And Hell is more terrible that what we can
                        imagine—   Matt 10:28
Jesus described it as darkness, gnashing of teeth, fire, and the
    ultimate separation from God
Jesus said people will be ultimately separated into two groups:
One entering into His presence (Heaven or paradise)—
The other banished to "eternal fire" (Hell)
These are the only two options (paths)
Moreover, we are spiritual beings with a soul and placed in
    physical bodies   Gen 2:7

And although our bodies will eventually die, Heb 9:27
Our souls and spirits are eternal Matt 25:46
They come from God; and hopefully they return to God
But if not, then they need another destination, called Hell
Jesus also said, "I am the way and the truth and the life.
No one comes to the Father except through me" John 14:6[17]
So, Jesus stands and waits at each landing that intersects with the escalator
He asks you to get off the escalator and "Follow Me" Luke 18:22
You need a Savior to avoid this destination
You need to be covered in the sinless blood, Jesus' blood
1 John 1:7
Jesus wants to be your Savior
But He gives you free will to choose (to decide) as your heart desires
If you ignore Him, then He continues to ask again at every landing below
Until there are no more floors left
He loves you more than anything else
That's why He keeps asking
If and once you agree, you exit the escalator
He leads you along the way; you simply follow Him
He leads you to another escalator
You step forward and are suddenly pulled upwards
Fortunately, there are no exits on this escalator
Once you are saved, you are forever saved John 10:27–28
Your destination, Heaven, has been decided and is permanent
You're on your way there
You made the right choice
Enjoy the ride

17. NIV.

This Life's a Test for All

(Adapted from the melody of "Physical" by Dua Lipa)

Our life is a strange construct fully understanding it's an obstacle
Our destiny is uncertainty

Is it some kind of system glitch, a higher power, or just by
    chance?
Is it sunny? Is it crappy? Nothing in this life will be perfect or
    guaranteed

It's not what you accrue
You can't take anything worldly with you once you're through
So, be warned, be warned, be warned   Ezek 3:21
This life's a test for all

With love, you're given a choice
Being human, saving ourselves is impossible—
    devoid   Eph 2:10–13
Be restored, restored, restored   Acts 3:19–21
This life's a test for all

Heaven's not a goal, but a destination
Not modification, but transformation   Rom 12:2
With charity and sincerity   Heb 10:22–23

The aim is to become more Christ-like   Rom 8:29
When His principles are applied
With faith and hope
Seek the kingdom of God first or you will be empty   Matt 6:33

Flesh dies, spirits renew   2 Cor 4:16
With patience and humility, you can undo   1 Pet 5:6–7
So, call on, call on, call on
This life's a test for all

Throughout, the road's a climb
But you can be a blessing one step at a time   Prov 11:25
So, bring on, bring on, bring on
This life's a test for all

Be a light in darkness, burn brighter   Matt 5:14–16
Be different from the world, extraordinary   John 15:19
Push on, try to keep on progressing
This life's a test for all

With practice, it becomes much lighter   Matt 11:30
Be real, be true; share the gospel directly   2 Tim 1:8
Go on, go on, go on
God's Word keeps professing   2 Tim 3:16
This life's a test for all

Proceed forward, keep sticking to
Despite any setbacks, you'll witness a breakthrough
So, belong, belong, belong
This life's a test for all

Check out, it's time to rejoice
You've accomplished your mission where you were deployed
                                                      2 Tim 4:7
So, you've won, you've won, you've won

This life's a test for all
This life's a test for all, test for all
This life's a test for all
This life's a, a, a test for all

Quiet Your Tongue

(Adapted from the melody of "Only the Young" by Taylor Swift)

Wish you could erase
It gives you disgrace   Matt 15:11
Sometimes it's used to accuse   Ps 52:2

It often divides   Prov 15:1
It frequently lies
There's no acceptable excuse

It can inflict, all others convict   Jas 3:2–10
Next time, consider to bite
You're so encumbered; make it right

Quiet your tongue, quiet your tongue   Prov 21:23
Quiet your tongue, quiet your tongue
Well done, well done; you've won, you've won, you've won

It knocks people down
It makes people frown
It can leave a lot of debris
In others' affairs, it always compares
All this, wouldn't you agree?

Instead, why not stand; pausing the plan
Why put your foot in your mouth?   Prov 21:23
For how quickly you'll regret

It makes you feel rebellious but later so helpless
You need to constrain this; you gotta say farewell
Try practicing composure over what's spoken
Then it turns contagious

Quiet your tongue, quiet your tongue
Quiet your tongue, quiet your tongue

Quiet your tongue, quiet your tongue
Quiet your tongue, quiet your tongue

Quiet your tongue, quiet your tongue
Quiet your tongue, quiet your tongue—well done

From now on, try to do what's right
The default of a mime   Prov 17:28
Expand your response time
You've won, you've won, you've won

Be careful when you opine   Jas 3:10
Think before you speak each time   Ps 37:30
And then things should be fine
You've won, you've won, you've won

Quiet your tongue, quiet your tongue, quiet your tongue

Don't Be a Hypocrite

(Adapted from the melody of "I Ain't Worried" by OneRepublic)

Careful of what you've been sold	
I'm here to speak the truth, in order to expose	
If judging others, you'll be judged	Matt 7:1
If done in public, there's no reward	Matt 6:3

Don't act like a hypocrite	Mark 7:6
You appear to thrive, but deep inside you're unclean	Titus 1:16
Don't act like a hypocrite	
You'll be punished because you're clearly frauds	

Don't be a hypocrite
Don't be a hypocrite

Fast, for others not to behold	
For what is unseen will be greater than gold	
What's fake will ultimately be exposed	
And true faith multiplied a hundredfold	Mark 4:20

The blind will lead the blind and their paths will be	
sealed	Matt 15:14
We'll know what they have not disclosed or have concealed	
They honor God with their lips, but their true nature	
revealed	Matt 23:27–28
They only deceive themselves for sure	

Don't act like a hypocrite
You appear to thrive, but deep inside you're unclean
Don't act like a hypocrite
You'll be punished because you're clearly frauds

Don't be a hypocrite
Don't be a hypocrite
Don't be a hypocrite

Don't act like a hypocrite
You appear to thrive, but deep inside you're unclean
Don't act like a hypocrite
You'll be punished because you're clearly frauds

Don't be a hypocrite
Don't be a hypocrite
Don't be a hypocrite

Finite

(Adapted from the melody of "Drive" by The Cars)

Wouldn't you recommend hearing it straight?
Or would you prefer instead just to debate?

You can't belong if you remain withdrawn; oh, oh
You don't know what you don't know—finite

Who do you plan to interrupt when you call?
Do you think it's just bad luck or someone's fault?

Would you ever seek redemption or is that too
    extreme?   Col 1:13–14
Who are you gonna cry to for help when you suffer disease

You can't belong if you remain withdrawn; oh, oh
You don't know what you don't know—finite

Will you still clown around with so much at stake?
Must you be knocked down to finally awake?   2 Cor 1:9

You can't belong if you remain withdrawn; oh, oh
You don't know what you don't know—finite

You can't belong if you remain withdrawn; oh, oh
You don't know what you don't know—finite

Mirror Image

A snowcapped mountain lines the horizon
The lake below is still
Another mountain points downward
Treacherous, but tranquil

What's the meaning of this mirror image?
It's splendor I'm thankful
But the consequences prove much more evident
Through the gift of free will

On one hand, God is found looking upwards   Ps 115:3
The third heaven's in the sky   2 Cor 12:2
Its beauty and expanse are truly awe-inspiring
With blessings if you apply

The other mountain range appears upside down
This is the path if one denies
It's a slippery slope filled with significance
You will stubble and slide

This dichotomy is as basic as it gets
Jesus will return as a lion   Rev 5:5
We're all mountaineers hiking to one of these destinations
Will it be Mount Sinai or Mount Zion?   Exod 19–24; Rev 14:1

Savior or Judge?

(Adapted from the melody of "Sure Thing" by Miguel)

Looking for another?
Who would you recommend?
There's only one to discover

Is He your Savior or judge and executioner?   Rom 10:9; Jas 4:12
Is He your Savior or judge and executioner?
Is He your Savior or judge and executioner?
Is He your Savior or judge and executioner?

You must be attached; Jesus Christ is the vine   John 15:5
And you're the branch, you'll have to choose
Eventually someday, but you can refuse
Yet that is simply crazy; and you might lose

Though undoubtedly your life will be mediocre
The Lord's Prayer is a misnomer
Talk the talk and walk the walk   Col 2:6
Or things will be awkward
Exist in the dark or doors can be unlocked

There's no more time for stalling
You don't want to be the punch line
You must fail so that you will resign   2 Cor 3:4–5
Surrender to Him and then things will align   Jas 4:7
Seek Him in all things and do it daily   1 Chr 22:19
Don't even bother with the question "Why?"
Don't drift through life lazily, you can ascertain
Otherwise, life will be mundane

Is He your Savior or judge and executioner?
Is He your Savior or judge and executioner?
Is He your Savior or judge and executioner?
Is He your Savior or judge and executioner?

You can choose to suffer; or have the desire to be saved
Or be corrupt, or have a provider—amazed
Learn to trust   Ps 33:4
Inspired maybe? You can bank on hope
If you're feeling it lately, you could gain the most
Unsurpassed

Light, there's a glimmer
Try, a beginner, and who knew?
From this world learning to detach

Later indeed, you might transcend
To overcome things in the end
Rely on Him, on Him depend   Isa 41:13; Prov 3:5–6

There's no more time for stalling
You don't want to be the punch line
You must fail so that you will resign
Surrender to Him and then things will align
Seek Him in all things and do it daily
Don't even bother with the question "Why?"
Don't drift through life lazily, you can ascertain
Otherwise, life will be mundane

If you want to be free namely
Let Him be in control, share your pleas plainly   1 Pet 5:7
Then walk with Him, saintly

Let Him guide you through the storms, guarantee
    your safety   Mark 4:35–41
If you want to experience His supply before you die, bravely
Jesus is our king, salvation He brings
And then living water will spring   John 7:37–39

There's no more time for stalling
You don't want to be the punch line
You must fail so that you will resign
Surrender to Him and then things will align
Seek Him in all things and do it daily
Don't even bother with the question "Why?"
Don't drift through life lazily, you can ascertain
Otherwise, life will be mundane

Looking for another?
Who would you recommend?
There's only one to discover

Did You Know?

Did you know that Jesus challenged the status quo   Matt 21:12–14
That He died about two thousand years ago   2 Pet 3:8
Just so that you can have a tomorrow?   Matt 6:34

Did you know that Satan suffered a deathblow   Gen 3:15
That Jesus armed you with special ammo   Acts 1:8
To have power over the enemy and then let go?   Acts 4:29–30
And did you know?

If you're not aware, you'll be harassed   Jas 1:2
You'll continue to fall under spiritual attacks   Eph 6:12
What you don't know will frequently trespass   1 Pet 5:8

If you're always waiting for a reply   Ps 37:7
If right away, you need a strong ally;   Ps 144:2
Everything you need, He'll supply   Phil 4:19

Did you know that Jesus challenged the status quo
That He died about two thousand years ago
Just so that you can have a tomorrow?

Did you know that Satan suffered a deathblow
That Jesus armed you with special ammo
To have power over the enemy and then let go?

If you still have a question mark
If you seek a brand-new adventure to embark
If life's so-so, call on the patriarch   Gen 12:1–3

You might want to try this technique
Visualize what you want and then speak   Gen 1:3; Ps 8:5
To avoid evil's clutch; your soul He'll keep   Ps 121:7–8

Did you know that Jesus challenged the status quo
That He died about two thousand years ago
Just so that you can have a tomorrow?

Did you know that Satan suffered a deathblow
That Jesus armed you with special ammo
To have power over the enemy and then let go?

And you have a foe who really hates you so   John 15: 18–20
And you have a foe who really hates you so
Well, did you know?

Did you know that Jesus challenged the status quo
That He died about two thousand years ago
Just so that you can have a tomorrow?

Did you know that Satan suffered a deathblow
That Jesus armed you with special ammo
To have power over the enemy and then let go?

Did you know that Jesus challenged the status quo
That He died about two thousand years ago
Just so that you can have a tomorrow?

Did you know that Satan suffered a deathblow
That Jesus armed you with special ammo
To have power over the enemy and then let go?
Well, now you know.

God Doesn't Send Anyone To Hell

(Adapted from the melody of "You Choose" by Pet Shop Boys)

Your thoughts, uncoerced	Isa 55:8–9
You determine	
Yes, you're the boss	
Your fate, it's true	
God doesn't send anyone to hell; you choose	2 Pet 3:9; Gal 5:13
Love is sent to you by the divine	1 John 4:16
You can accept this	Josh 24:15
Or you can decline	
There's just one chance	
Just one lifeline	
Or darkness and despair you'll find	Rom 13:2
He whoever hears	Rom 10:9–10
and believes this thought	
Will gain eternal life	
and thus, not be judged	Rom 8:1–34
But why descend?	
You can become brand new	2 Cor 5:17
You can be redeemed	1 Pet 1:3–5
Jesus in lieu	2 Cor 5:14
If only you knew	
But now you do	Matt 12:36
This human existence	
You're just passing through	Heb 9:27; 1 John 5:11
How fleeting your life is	
Permanent consequences	Prov 5: 1–23
will soon loom	
Why would you defer	
and instead, wince?	
He chose to love you despite your sin	Rom 5:8

Fear the Father	Ps 34:9; Rev 14:7
Note His woes	Luke 6:24–26
God doesn't send anyone to hell, you know	
You can't right the wrongs	Ps 49:7–9
There's no excuse	Rom 1:20
God doesn't send anyone to hell; you choose	

Stubbornness

(Adapted from the melody of "Loneliness" by Pet Shop Boys)

This is your final chance	
To express what's in your heart	
Accept or deny My Holiness	Lev 20:26
You must choose before you depart	Jer 21:8

How are you gonna hide from My Holiness?	Prov 15:3
My Holiness	
Why do you hold onto your stubbornness?	Jer 18:12
Stubbornness	

Your recent cancer diagnosis	
And your dear son's frequent moans	
Your fear of needles and now disease relapse	
All of these things have been made known	Rom 1:20

How are you gonna escape from My Holiness?
My Holiness
Why do you think you can avoid My final judgment?
Judgment

When are you gonna reject atheism, surrender, and	
just confess?	Gal 5:24–25
Your time is quickly running out	Rom 13:11
Soon—eternal distress	Rev 21:8

The biological sciences have brainwashed you	
Everything has been a lie	John 8:44
You've been deceived by Satan, by pride	Jas 4:6
In hell, you'll forever reside	Matt 25:31–46

You've been poisoned by groupthink	
But you can be forgiven by Jesus' blood	Eph 1:7

How are you gonna hide from My Holiness?
My Holiness
Why do you hold onto your stubbornness?
Stubbornness

When are you gonna reject atheism, surrender, and just confess?
Your time is quickly running out
Soon—eternal distress

Stubbornness, stubbornness
Stubbornness, stubbornness
Stubbornness, stubbornness
Stubbornness, stubbornness

How are you gonna escape My Holiness?
My Holiness
Why do you think you can avoid My final judgment?
Judgment

How are you gonna hide from My Holiness?
My Holiness
Why do you hold onto your stubbornness?
Stubbornness

When are you gonna reject atheism, surrender, and just confess?
Your time is quickly running out
Soon—eternal distress

Stubbornness
Stubbornness
Stubbornness
Stubbornness

PRAYER

Prayer is Stronger than the Vaccine

(Adapted from the melody of "A Dream of You and Me" by Future Islands)

I'm sick of this enemy
My hidden identity
Behind a mask visibly
This needs to end desperately
No more helplessly

All of us have lost control
Just a new normal, I suppose
Living our lives just to avoid getting exposed
In every city, lockdowns imposed

Some struggle breathlessly
We need some clarity
We're damaged mentally
And spaced apart six feet
This is not our destiny

Each of us fears the unknown
Our futures can't be postponed
Loss of freedom, loss of liberty—we must condone
We're not designed to be alone

Can you wait, can you wait for the vaccine?
Can you wait, can you wait for the vaccine?
Can you wait, can you wait for the vaccine?
Can you wait, can you wait for the vaccine?

We're all . . . withdrawn
We're all . . . withdrawn

I received the vaccine
I received the vaccine
I received the vaccine
I received the vaccine

I received the vaccine
I found an escape for me
Praying on my knees   Eph 3:14–21

The Secret

(Adapted from the melody of "Pocketful of Sunshine" by Natasha Bedingfield)

The LORD's my boss, He directs all my thoughts
He's figured out how to get His point across, oh-oh
I've learned so much, I've decided to be carefree
Show your fruit, don't be like the fig tree, oh, oh-oh Matt 21:18–22

The LORD's my boss, He directs all my thoughts
He's figured out how to get His point across, oh-oh
When I'm down and when I'm feeling lonely
I ask openly that He will show me now, oh-oh   Ps 143:8

When things are grey, as they decay
Begin to pray; He'll make a way   1 Thess 5:16–18
He'll make a way with words He'll say   Gen 1:3
Without delay, a better day

Here's the secret that shows just how His grace will flow
May I propose that you must disclose
That He is the light of the world and despite   John 8:12
What others write; this you must recite   Rom 10:9

When things are grey, as they decay
Begin to pray; He'll make a way
He'll make a way with words He'll say
Without delay, a better day

The LORD will provide, let Him be your guide   Phil 4:19
Trust that He'll reside deep down inside   1 John 4:12–14
And that He'll supply all things if you comply   Phil 4:19
This you must decide; your fears will subside   1 John 4:18

When things are grey, as they decay
Begin to pray; He'll make a way
He'll make a way with words He'll say
Without delay, a better day

When things are grey, as they decay
Begin to pray; He'll make a way
He'll make a way with words He'll say
Without delay, a better day

MUST

Whenever you pray, don't be like the hypocrites	Matt 6:5
Standing tall, preaching loud to all	
But rather you MUST do so quietly	Matt 6:18
Whoever wants to be great MUST become a servant	
	Matt 20:28
The gospel MUST be preached to all	Matt 28:19–20
Not law, but grace described by Paul	Eph 2:8–9

With most certainty, you MUST be born again	John 3:5–7
Truly if you want to ascend	
To be with Me always in Heaven	Daniel 2:28
Be prepared for the end, you MUST be ready	
Because the Son of Man will return to earth	Matt 24:30–31
At an hour unexpectedly	Matt 24:36–44

Don't you know, don't you know?
I MUST be in My Father's House; I MUST be in My Father's
    House   John 14:2–6

You will hear of wars and even more rumors of wars	Matt 24:6
Oh no, oh no!	

Make sure that you are not alarmed	
Everything written MUST be fulfilled	Isa 53:5
For all of this MUST occur	

You certainly MUST practice forgiveness	Matt 6:14–15
Even if he sins against you seven times	Matt 18: 21–22
And seven more he returns	

Don't you know, don't you know?
I MUST be in My Father's House; I MUST be in My Father's
    House

You MUST worship me in spirit and in truth
I MUST be in My Father's House

You MUST be perfect, in the sense that I am
If you are in Christ,   Gal 3:27–28
Then you are too
The Son of Man MUST be lifted up   John 3: 14–16
You are righteous   2 Cor 5:21
A gift I gave to you   John 3:16

Save Me

(Adapted from the melody of "Hate Me" by Ellie Goulding & Juice WRLD)

Save me, save me; peace and calm escape me	Ps 119:146
Wake me, wake me; please don't forsake me	Ps 38:21
Embrace me, embrace me; fix my destination	John 3:16
Claim me, claim me; so that I don't betray thee	Matt 10:32–33

I have to learn to stop being opposed	
I always want to feel like I'm in control	
I'm not comfortable with being so exposed	
It's like I'm dead and starting to decompose	Rom 6:10–12

I wish I could do more than just complain	
Although You're God, I know that You can relate	John 1:14
So, Jesus; you have the power to recreate	2 Cor 5:17
So, maybe I'll put all my faith in You and just wait	Acts 16:31

Why don't You save me, save me; peace and calm escape me
Wake me, wake me; please don't forsake me
Embrace me, embrace me; fix my destination
Claim me, claim me; so that I don't betray thee

Save me, save me; peace and calm escape me
Wake me, wake me; please don't forsake me
Embrace me, embrace me; fix my destination
Claim me, claim me; so that I don't betray thee

Save me, save me; peace and calm escape me	
I know I'm not too far gone; I feel close strangely	Jas 4:8
I harbor all the blame; I know You won't give up on me	Rev 3:20
It might be because of my magnified self-worth, I'm vain	
It might be because of an undiagnosed mental illness, I'm insane	
I want to be part of Your heaven's eternal domain	Ps 16:11
I don't want to be left behind or left to remain	

I always want to be with You and proclaim Your name   2 Cor 4

Take me, break me, purposefully reshape me   Isa 64:8
Cleanse me of my tears, please carry me safely   Rev 21:4
I hope You see my worth, please accommodate me   2 Thess 1:11
Salvation You bring   Acts 16:31

Save me, save me; peace and calm escape me
Wake me, wake me; please don't forsake me
Embrace me, embrace me; fix my destination
Claim me, claim me; so that I don't betray thee

Save me, save me; peace and calm escape me
Wake me, wake me; please don't forsake me
Embrace me, embrace me; fix my destination
Claim me, claim me; so that I don't betray thee

I wish I could do more than just complain
Although You're God, I know that You can relate
So, Jesus; you have the power to recreate
So, maybe I'll put all my faith in You and just wait

Why don't You save me, save me; peace and calm escape me
Wake me, wake me; please don't forsake me
Embrace me, embrace me; fix my destination
Claim me, claim me; so that I don't betray thee

Save me, save me; peace and calm escape me
Wake me, wake me; please don't forsake me
Embrace me, embrace me; fix my destination
Claim me, claim me; so that I don't betray thee

Tell me that You'll save me
Claim me, claim me; so that I don't betray thee
Tell me that You'll save me
Claim me, claim me; so that I don't betray thee

A Listening Heart

(Adapted from the melody of "Record Player" by Daisy the Great &
AJR)

Waiting in silence was always difficult for me
But developing a listening heart is what is needed   1 Kgs 3:9–28
If you want to talk with God and hear His expertise
It'll come as a whisper since He's inside of thee   1 Kgs 19

Waiting in silence was always difficult for me
But developing a listening heart is what is needed
If you want to talk with God and hear His expertise
It'll come as a whisper since He's inside of thee

It involves meditation—you have to calm way down   Josh 1:8
Slow your breathing and listen to every sound
It's profound

Remain still and see what it shall bring   Josh 1:8
It takes practice and feels sort of unbecoming

You might not hear anything for a while
But with time, it'll become fertile
Then out of the blue, it'll befall
You might yawn, but keep on

Waiting in silence was always difficult for me
But developing a listening heart is what is needed
If you want to talk with God and hear His expertise
It'll come as a whisper since He's inside of thee

Waiting in silence was always difficult for me
But developing a listening heart is what is needed
If you want to talk with God and hear His expertise
It'll come as a whisper since He's inside of thee

You're your own cultivator; set aside time to pray   Dan 6:10
Share your hidden concerns with Him and then obey   1 Pet 5:7;
                                                                                    John 14:15–31
Everyday
Don't forget to offer Him praise   Isa 25:1
Be positive with any delay
Yes, not now, or denied: He will answer you someday   Matt 7:7–8

You might not hear anything for a while
But with time, it'll become fertile
Make your request known and then some   1 Pet 5:7
And when He answers—awestruck

Waiting in silence was always difficult for me
But developing a listening heart is what is needed
If you want to talk with God and hear His expertise
It'll come as a whisper since He's inside of thee

Waiting in silence was always difficult for me
But developing a listening heart is what is needed
If you want to talk with God and hear His expertise
It'll come as a whisper since He's inside of thee

Approach with honor, respect, and submission   Jas 4:7
Be humble when you seek the divine   Prov 29:23
An outward sign of your inward condition
Do it in a position of reverence down on your knees   Eph 3:14–2

THE GIFT OF LIFE

Precious Life

(Adapted from the melody of "Creeping" by The Weeknd & 21 Savage)

There's no one else like you	1 Pet 2:9
I breathed life into you and then you came to be	Gen 2:7
You simply didn't evolve from goo	
Your spirit in flesh debuted	Gen 1:26

This occurred long ago	Gen 1:31
I knew you in the womb as an embryo	Jer 1:5
I'm hidden inside you, incognito	1 John 4:12–13
Satan's misleading today and tomorrow	John 8:44
As it's written in My manifesto	John 1:1

It's true; for Satan has confused the truth	
Don't fall for his lies; you were conceived	John 8:44
Given a precious life to choose	Gen 2:7
There's another realm concealed	2 Cor 12–13

This occurred long ago
I knew you in the womb as an embryo
I'm hidden inside you, incognito
Satan's misleading today and tomorrow
As it's written in My manifesto

You are so very special to Me; I made you to be unique	Ps 139:13–14
I designed you to be eternal; My chosen appointee	Eph 1:4–5
My Son's the only doorway; we'll be reunited someday	John 14:6
You're a spirit being; I can set you free	Gal 5:1

It's not trivial, you're not destined to be extinct	
Your human lifespan will be gone within a blink	
You are given two paths with only one to choose	
It's true; you were purposefully hand-picked	Eph 1:4–11

Please don't just aimlessly wander astray   Num 22:1
This is serious, please don't shrug off or downplay
This is about eternity, possibly your doomsday
In the pit of hell, you'll be sentenced forever to decay   Rev 20:15

Now is the time, please don't continue to postpone
You can have eternal life despite your tombstone
If you refuse; in the Lake of Fire, you'll be thrown   Rev 20:15
Ongoing torment, this to endlessly bemoan

This occurred long ago
I knew you in the womb as an embryo
I'm hidden inside you, incognito
Satan's misleading today and tomorrow
As it's written in My manifesto

I knew you in the womb as an embryo
I'm hidden inside you, incognito
Satan's misleading today and tomorrow
As it's written in My manifesto

Believe in Me; rebuke Satan and denounce him   Matt 4:10
Satan's goal is to betray   Rev 20:10
Be careful; seek Me and always pray   1 Thess 5:16–18
I will bring great things; this I can guarantee   John 3:16

Her Cries Ignored

Nothing is heard, but ripples felt
No tears are shed except for guilt
Her cries are muffled and ignored
Forsaken she's been of being born

Denied her life because we say
A gift from God stripped away   Ps 127:3
She cries all night and through the day
Soon, she'll be no more

Toss and turn, she pleas again
With kicks and stabs, wake up she sends
Her mom's afraid and her dad's disturbed
Of what will happen if she is heard

Denied her life because we say
A gift from God stripped away
She cries all night and through the day
Soon, she'll be no more

The day is here, a silent step
Two uneasy souls filled with regret   Exod 20:13
We're dragged with demons down to hell
A staircase traveled that once repelled

Denied her life because we say
A gift from God stripped away
She cries all night and through the day
Soon, she'll be no more

While at home, we start to mourn
About the little one who wasn't born
Anger, disgust, tears, and shame
A piece of us lost still without a name   Jer 1:5

Denied her life because we say
A gift from God stripped away
She cries all night and through the day
Until we'll be no more

Years have passed, the scars repressed
We've asked of Him His forgiveness   1 John 1:9
Denied, we're due; damned, we accept
'Cause we broke His trust with silent steps
Denied her life because we say
A gift from God stripped away
She cries all night and through the day
Until we'll be no more

As each day ends, we pray some more   1 Thess 5:16–18
Remorseful of her cries ignored   Acts 2:38
And though we live in fear and faith
We continue to seek His absent grace

Denied her life because we say
A gift from God stripped away
Cherished and loved, life must remain   Jer 31:3
Soon, we may become free   Rom 8:1–2

BLESSINGS

To Be A Friend

To be a friend, you have to care
Stand next to someone and always be there
Adding support, and never abort
That special someone when they have been scared

To be a friend, you have to love
To carry them with you to places above
Showing the way, their trust does not betray
For you they depend; on your hand, their glove

To be a friend, you have to share
Making sacrifices for the weights you bear
Always listen to make them glisten
And to hold them close if you should dare

To be a friend, you are a gift
To help them understand, their sadness you lift
Pain, you receive; in them, you believe
Walking together on life's path, you drift

To be a friend means to give faith
Hope and strength you bring them whatever they face
Nothing revised and nothing disguised
You are true to them; in their heart, your place

Counting My Blessings

With memories to look back upon
To see the reason why I am here
I reflect on those who have helped me out
With the battle to overcome my fears

To do this, I consider a painting
But more soon the colors of its paints
This indeed helps me count all of my blessings
On this November day for giving thanks

And as I reflect back on my life
I closely listen to those who care
I can see truly how lucky I am
Because of all their insights which they have shared

So, as we look to one another
The beautiful humans that we are
We shouldn't necessarily look on the surface
For on the inside is who we really are

You see, humans are like paintings
They are for admiration, just like saints
We can experience all their beauty and mystery
But to do so, we must focus on the colors of their paints

Now with these ideas fixed in your heads
I can point out my colors from where they stem
So, look, and look closely, but not at my painting
But look at the inside which makes me who I am

These are the colors of my paints:

I've been blessed with a love who cares for me with all her heart
So special she is to me; a very important part

I've been blessed with a study to donate myself to others
To function in their lives for my sisters and my brothers

I've been blessed with my health; alive and full of function
Stronger for the future and stronger for the structure
I've been blessed with a smile to laugh and show my teeth
Encouraging other giggles and to make stronger for the weak

I've been blessed with a family who adds support every day
They're always there in need and they're never far away
I've been blessed with education to enhance my knowledge and
   skills
To use throughout my life through the obstacles and the drills

I've been blessed with direction to choose and follow my own
   dreams
No matter what they are and no matter where they lead
I've been blessed with my friends who accept me and my ways
Friendship they supply throughout the nights and all the days

I've been blessed with my writings for poems are what I do best
Letting people read my thoughts as I do not stand upon the fence

I've been blessed with all these gifts   1 Cor 12:4–11
So fruitful, and so many   Matt 7:15–20
To give all of myself to persons—all and any

So, here are the blessings which I count
They are the colors of my paints
Yet, I do not give credit to myself   Jas 1:17; 1 Cor 12:1–1
For it is all of these that I do give thanks

So, as we look to one another
The beautiful humans that we are
We shouldn't necessarily look on the surface
For on the inside is who we really are

About the Author

Eric Zack is a born-again Christian who resorted to poetry as his preferred emotional outlet at the age of twenty years old. At that time, his dear mother died from metastatic cancer at the age of thirty-nine years old. His mother's cancer was not directly talked about in the open with him or his three younger brothers, although she was diagnosed several years before her death. He was raised in a stable middle-class home environment in a small town in the middle of the United States in the Roman Catholic faith and served as an altar boy for several years growing up. He had a difficult time processing what had happened and stepped away from his faith temporarily as he coped and adjusted with this "new normal." Fortunately, he soon returned to his faith with a renewed passion to develop a closer relationship with his Savior Jesus Christ while trying to better understand life, suffering, loss, and healing. His personal mission statement and professional goals have been to "make a difference and help others" because he was not able to do so for his mother.

Since a young age, Eric has generally possessed an introvert personality type and has often kept his thoughts and feelings private for the most part until now. He is also an experienced and expert oncology nurse and nursing college professor in response to his mom's death, which occurred during his third year of college. Today, he is married and has four adult children, none of whom have ever met his mother. Eric's poetry has dealt with most aspects of living life and covers many different, unique topics that most human beings will experience. More recently, he has been driven to write about many aspects of his maturing Christian faith. He noted a significant gap in the literature in regard to Christian poetry that is supported by the Holy Bible and the many truths that the Holy Bible shares. As a result, he wanted to publish his poetry collections to share with whomever is interested in learning more about these topics, whomever enjoys reading and meditating on various Bible verses, and whomever enjoys poetry in general. He felt it a priority at this time in his life to pursue publishing these five volumes to help others in their spiritual journeys given today's serious crises and waning timeline.

His other poetry collections that are not directly related to Christianity may be published at a future date. Eric's poetry style is typically rhythmic and rhyming in nature with repeated chorus lines (almost like a song) to support certain important aspects worth stressing. Up to this point, his poems have been hidden from all and considered amateur (never shared or published before). This has been his "quiet" passion for over thirty years now; and he hopes that some good may come out of him sharing these authentic, cherished poems that are very personal and private in nature. He sincerely believes that the Holy Spirit has coauthored most of these, using him as a vessel to reach others who are in desperate need of answers and/or support.

Thank you for allowing small pieces of me and my life's insight into your reality and life. And may Jesus Christ have all the power, praise, and glory for doing so. And may God continue to bless you and your loved ones as you seek to get closer and closer to Him. In Christ Jesus, Eric.